WILLIAM HOWARD TAFT

ENCYCLOPEDIA of PRESIDENTS

William Howard Taft

Twenty-Seventh President of the United States

By Jane Clark Casey

Consultant: Charles Abele, Ph.D.
Social Studies Instructor
Chicago Public School System

CHILDRENS PRESS®
CHICAGO

Taft and family at Murray Bay during his Supreme Court years

To my cherished mother and unfailing friend, Rita Maus Carfagno.

Library of Congress Cataloging-in-Publication Data

Casey, Jane Clark.
    William Howard Taft.

    (Encyclopedia of presidents)
    Includes index.
    Summary: Examines the life and career of the lawyer
whose relatively unsuccessful presidency was followed by
a happy term as Chief Justice of the Supreme Court.
    1.   Taft, William H. (William Howard), 1857-1930—
Juvenile literature.   2.   Presidents—United States—
Biography—Juvenile literature.   3.   United States—
Politics and government—1901-1909—Juvenile literature.
4.   United States—Politics and government—1909-1913—
Juvenile literature.   [1.   Taft, William H. (William
Howard), 1857-1930.   2.   Presidents]   I. Title.   II. Series.
E762.C37   1989   973.91'2'0924   [B]   [92]   88-8675
ISBN 0-516-01366-1

Picture Acknowledgments

AP/Wide World Photos—5, 32, 48 (bottom), 60,
68 (bottom), 69 (top), 75, 86, 87 (2 pictures), 88
(bottom)

The Bettmann Archive, Inc.—23, 24, 25, 48
(top), 61, 63, 64, 68 (top), 69 (bottom), 70 (top),
88 (top), 89

Historical Pictures Service, Chicago—6, 8, 31, 38
(top), 39 (bottom), 43, 49 (2 pictures), 50
(bottom), 56, 57 (2 pictures), 58, 62, 71, 72

Library of Congress—29, 50 (top), 51 (top), 52,
76, 83

National Park Service: Statue of Liberty National
Monument—70 (bottom)

Supreme Court Historical Society—80

William Howard Taft National Historic Site—4,
10, 12, 13 (2 pictures), 14, 15, 17 (2 pictures),
18, 21, 22, 26, 28, 30, 34, 38 (bottom), 39 (top),
40, 44

U.S. Bureau of Printing and Engraving—2

Cover design and illustration
by Steven Gaston Dobson

Chief Justice Taft in
1922 with former U.S.
Supreme Court justice
Oliver Wendell Holmes

Table of Contents

Chapter 1

A Reluctant Warrior

It was April of 1912 and spring had come, even to chilly New England. Each time the little train came to a stop, President William Howard Taft emerged to tell the cheering crowds how much he needed their votes and their help in governing the nation for another four years. In each speech, he complained bitterly of former president Theodore Roosevelt's attacks. Taft said that Roosevelt, who was campaigning against him for the Republican nomination, was telling lies about his record. He claimed Roosevelt was not giving him the "square deal" that Roosevelt himself always demanded.

His listeners knew that Taft and Roosevelt had once been allies, but that Roosevelt had long since split with Taft. They knew that Roosevelt was openly criticizing the president, but that Taft had let the attacks go unanswered. It must have seemed to them that spring day that Taft had finally become self-confident enough and angry enough to turn openly on his former friend. Actually, Taft was miserable. A reporter who approached him as the train returned to Washington found him bowed over, his head in his hands, weeping. He looked up and explained, "Roosevelt was my closest friend."

One of many political
cartoons published during
Taft's unsuccessful run
for reelection in 1912

The truth was that Taft detested conflict. His mother, Louise Torrey Taft, knew this about him and had warned him against pursuing the presidency in the first place. In 1907, when others were encouraging him to make his first run for the office, she sensed his reluctance and wrote to him: "So near the throne, you realize that 'Uneasy lies the head that wears the crown.' . . . The malice of politics would make you miserable. They do not want you as their leader, but cannot find anyone more available."

During the heated 1906 congressional campaigns, Taft had admitted privately, "Politics, when I'm in it, makes me sick." Had he listened to his mother and to his own heart, he would have turned his back on the presidency and been remembered as an honored statesman and judge. Instead, he is known primarily as an unsuccessful president who was soundly rejected when he ran for reelection. His four years in the presidency were hardly a disaster for the nation, but they were easily the worst years of his life.

Taft was a kindly, jovial man with an excellent judicial mind. He possessed unquestioned integrity and a vast sympathy for human problems. A patient and effective administrator, he achieved national honor and public confidence as governor of the Philippines just after America acquired control of those islands. As secretary of war under Roosevelt, he made up for his aversion to conflict. Displaying remarkable skill, he brought warring parties into agreement. After leaving the presidency, he served with distinction as chief justice of the Supreme Court. Yet the very qualities that brought him these successes—the genial nature, the reluctance to fight, the sense of honor, the judicial temperament—all contributed to the many mistakes of his political life. These qualities were particularly significant in shaping his failures as president.

Taft let his ambitious wife and brothers push him beyond his abilities and into the presidency. While they were almost certainly trying to give him good advice, it was his mother who understood him best. In 1907, when Taft was considered the front runner for the Republican nomination for president, a reporter jokingly asked Louise Taft whom she supported for president. She shocked the young man by responding, "Elihu Root." She went on to explain that her son belonged on the Supreme Court, rather than in the presidency. If Taft's other advisers had been as perceptive as she, American history might have taken a very different turn.

Chapter 2

A Promising Young Man

Though born and reared in Cincinnati, Ohio, William Howard Taft was shaped more by New England than by the Midwest. His ancestors on both sides were from Massachusetts and Vermont. His father, Alphonso Taft, chose both his first wife, who died young, and William's mother from eastern families. Both Alphonso's family and that of Louise Torrey Taft were well-respected and prosperous.

Alphonso served two terms as a superior court judge in Cincinnati. He was both secretary of war and attorney general under President Ulysses S. Grant. He later ran, without success, as the Republican candidate for governor of Ohio in 1879.

William, who was born September 15, 1857, had two older half-brothers, Charles and Peter, who had been born to Alphonso's first wife, Fanny Phelps. These boys both treated him, all their lives, with the love and protection they would have offered a full brother. He had two younger brothers, Henry and Horace, and a sister, Fanny Louise. The Taft family lived in a gracious but not showy home on Mount Auburn, which was separated by green fields and lots from the bustling commerce of the city below. Though Cincinnati at that time was already losing ground to Saint Louis and Chicago in terms of industry and population, it remained a center of river traffic and a lively and cultured city.

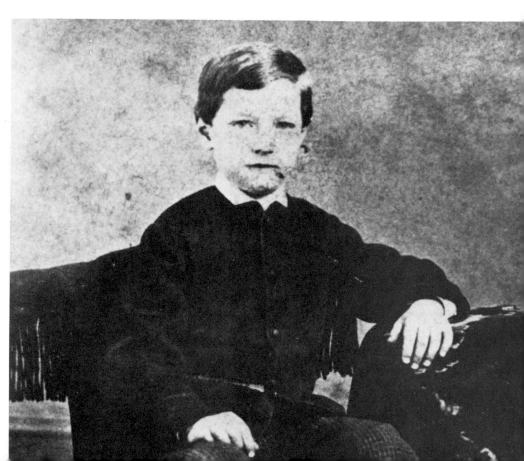

Opposite page: Louise Taft
and baby William ("Winnie")

Right: Alphonso Taft

Below: William at the
age of six

Taft (sitting, with hat on) in high school

Tall, attractive, and athletic, Taft was a popular boy who did well in high school, where he finished second in his class. He started dancing lessons at age twelve, did very well, and remained an excellent dancer all his life. Though William was plump, he was not seriously overweight during his youth. His twinkly blue eyes, easy laugh, and pleasant disposition made him popular wherever he went.

From the time he was a young boy, William had his heart set on attending Yale University in New Haven, Connecticut. Alphonso had graduated from Yale, and some of William's earliest memories were of his father's stories about the traditions of Yale. He enrolled in the fall of

Taft (in doorway, center) with his Yale graduating class

1874. At Alphonso's insistence, he gave up the sports he loved in order to focus on studies. He did not smoke or drink, but he disliked chapel, complaining that it combined hard benches with dry sermons. Despite this irreverent attitude, he did well at Yale and won admission to the exclusive Skull & Bones Society. Finishing second in his class of 132, he delivered the class oration.

William enrolled in Cincinnati Law School in the fall of 1878, but seems not to have approached law school with the single-mindedness he had devoted to Yale. Throughout his legal studies, he worked as a reporter on the Cincinnati *Commercial*, where he was assigned to cover the courts.

During at least some of this period, Taft was distracted by the charms of Helen Herron (called "Nellie"), whom he met at a coasting party in 1879, when Nellie was eighteen. During the early 1880s, Nellie began hosting regular gatherings at which books were discussed. Will was a regular, and he and Nellie developed a very intellectual friendship. Though they occasionally went out together, he was still addressing her, as late as April of 1884, as "My dear Miss Herron."

By April of 1885, however, he had worked up the courage to propose. She rejected him, but this was common for well-bred girls of the time. It may have had nothing to do with her actual feelings toward William. In May of that same year, he wrote to her: "Oh Nellie, do say that you will try to love me. Oh, how I will work and strive to be better and do better, how I will labor for our joint advancement if you will only let me." She finally consented, and they married on June 19, 1886.

Throughout their years together, Taft really did strive, just as he had promised, to reject his easygoing inclinations and labor for their joint advancement. Like his father, Taft preferred intelligent and challenging women. In Nellie, he had found his dream. She was bright, musical, ambitious, and very much inclined to take charge. She pushed him through all their life together and challenged him whenever she disagreed. He rarely made any significant decision without her advice. Indeed, he might well have accomplished much less in life without her encouragement. They ultimately had three children, Robert Alphonso, Helen Herron, and Charles Phelps.

Above: Taft's birthplace, Mount Auburn, in Cincinnati, Ohio
Below: Taft (center) and his future wife (seated, right) at a literary gathering

Chapter 3

A Life of Public Service Begins

Taft was licensed to practice law in 1880. He continued to work for the *Commercial*, however, until he was appointed assistant prosecutor of Hamilton County, at a salary of $1,200 a year, in October 1880. He held some public office for almost all the rest of his life. Taft was a diligent worker, both in his job and for the Republican party in Ohio.

In 1882, President Chester A. Arthur appointed him tax collector for the Cincinnati district, which made Taft the youngest such collector in the country. He was, however, immediately asked to fire some employees whom he considered to be reliable, dutiful, and energetic. He declined to do such "dirty work" and resigned shortly thereafter to go into the private practice of law. He briefly combined private practice with work as assistant county solicitor of Hamilton County. In March of 1887, Governor Joseph B. Foraker appointed him to fill a vacancy on the Ohio Superior Court. Though only twenty-nine at the time, he performed well and was easily elected to a full term in 1888.

In July of 1889, Foraker and other Republican party leaders urged President Benjamin Harrison to appoint Taft to the United States Supreme Court. Apparently the appointment was seriously considered, in spite of Taft's youth. Taft was excited at the prospect, but he saw little hope of actually getting the appointment. He wrote to his father, "My chances of going to the moon and of donning a silk gown [a judge's robe] at the hands of President Harrison are about equal."

Taft was not nominated for the Supreme Court spot, but Harrison did offer him the post of solicitor general. The solicitor general is the federal government's own lawyer, ranking second only to the attorney general. Though he had been eager for appointment to the Supreme Court, Taft was nervous about the job as solicitor general. Had Nellie not encouraged him, he might well have declined.

Another concern was finances: the job paid only $7,000 per year, and Taft was not sure he could support Nellie and the children on that amount in Washington, D.C. His brother Charles came to the rescue, as he was to do many times in Taft's life. He promised to supplement the family income as needed. With that assurance, Taft accepted the appointment and was sworn in in February 1890. He was only thirty-two years old. It was during Taft's term as solicitor general that he met Theodore Roosevelt, who was to play such an important role in his political future.

It was also during this period, on May 21, 1891, that Alphonso Taft died. Thus Taft lost a person who might have been one of his best sources of guidance and support through the thorny paths of politics.

Taft around the age of thirty-three

Though he was an efficient and respected solicitor general, Taft asked his friends in 1892 to recommend his appointment as U.S. circuit judge for the Sixth Circuit. This was the highest federal court position next to Supreme Court justice.

He was sworn in to that position on March 21, 1892. It was one of the rare occasions when he made a career move over Nellie's objections: she would have preferred him to stay in Washington with what she described as "the big wigs." The Tafts were able to live once again in Cincinnati, where they could live comfortably on his $6,000-a-year salary. As a circuit judge, Taft himself had to travel widely through Ohio, Kentucky, Michigan, and Tennessee.

Taft in his robes as federal circuit court judge

This was one of the happiest periods in Taft's life. He became a noted and influential circuit court judge, and in 1895 was again mentioned as a candidate for the Supreme Court. It was a period in which he could delight in his children and in Nellie, to whom he was devoted. His correspondence with her as he traveled the circuit is delightful; it displays his admiration for her as an intellectual equal. In 1895, he wrote to her, "You are my dearest and best critic and are worth much to me in stirring me up to

Helen Herron Taft, known as "Nellie"

best endeavor." It was also during this period that the
family began vacationing in Murray Bay, on the St. Lawrence River in Canada. Murray Bay remained the family's
summer retreat for most of the rest of Taft's life. Only
during his years as president, when he thought it inap-
propriate to vacation outside the country, did he choose
another summer home. Around Murray Bay he was known
as *"le petit juge"*—"the little judge"—and the locals
tipped their hats to him when he rode by.

Parade of striking railroad men in Cincinnati

Unfortunately for Taft, however, this was also the beginning of his public image as an enemy of labor unions. Though he believed in the right of workers to unite, he was frightened by the violence connected with the labor movement. He did not seem to understand that labor could not bargain equally with management without legal protection. He held unions to the letter of the law. For instance, a railroad whose employees were on strike came to him when other railroads, fearing strikes by their own employees, refused to carry its freight. The railroad wanted an injunction (order) compelling these other railroads to carry its freight. Taft granted the injunction, believing that the union's threat to hold other strikes was unlawful. He also imprisoned a labor leader, Frank Phelan, for encouraging a secondary boycott—that is, a boycott of a company doing business with the employer who was the target of the strike. At the same time, he was

Militia keep strikers away from mills in Lawrence, Massachusetts, to prevent violence.

quite protective of employees' personal safety. He once refused to honor a contract in which an employee had given up his right to receive money for injuries suffered at work. Another time, he rejected an argument that an employee had accepted the risk of injury by remaining at work that he knew was dangerous.

Taft also brought new life into the Sherman Antitrust Act during this period. This law made it illegal for any company to control the price or the distribution of goods. The act had been interpreted so narrowly by other courts—including the Supreme Court—that it had become almost meaningless. When a group of pipe manufacturers were charged with conspiring to keep the price of pipe high, however, Taft ruled that this was a conspiracy to control the *sale* of an item rather than its manufacture. He was thus able to order an end to the conspiracy without directly attacking the Supreme Court's position.

Chapter 4

Governing the Philippines

As Taft enjoyed his happy life on the court, events in which he had little interest were about to change that life. In 1898, the United States had been engaged in the Spanish-American War. It was during this war that Theodore Roosevelt became a national hero as the leader of the "Rough Riders." In the treaty with Spain that ended the war, the United States acquired the Philippine Islands.

Taft had given little thought to the Philippines except to oppose their annexation. He was thunderstruck when President McKinley called him by cable to Washington in 1900 and asked him to join the commission that would govern the islands. "He might as well have told me," Taft later wrote, "that he wanted me to take a flying machine." Once again unsure of his ability to do the job, he turned to Nellie and his brothers for advice. They urged him to take the job. So did his friend Elihu Root, who was McKinley's secretary of war. With that encouragement, he finally agreed.

Opposite page: Taft meets with Vatican officials about the Philippine friars.

Taft with his wife and son Charles in the Philippines

As president of the Philippine Commission, and later as civil governor of the islands, Taft was an enormous success. Both McKinley and Vice-President Roosevelt came to think of him as indispensable. He arrived in the Philippines in the summer of 1900 and immediately set out to acquire as much information as possible about the islands. The task was enormous. There are more than seven thousand islands in the Philippines and, at the time of Taft's arrival, the residents spoke at least seven main languages and countless dialects. Though no census had ever been taken, it was estimated that there were about seven million inhabitants in the islands.

Taft quickly came to admire the Filipino people. He rejected the American military's notion that they were incapable of governing themselves. Deftly he maneuvered

Democrat William Jennings Bryan in an 1896 photograph

to have actual control of the islands moved from the military to the commission. He included Filipinos in all official entertainments. He was careful not to criticize the revolutionary leaders who still threatened the fragile peace. To avoid being linked with wealthy urban Filipinos, he traveled extensively throughout the islands.

Taft's principal goal was to give Filipinos the greatest possible control over their own affairs. He did not view the islands as immediately capable of self-governance, however, and suppressed publications that advocated independence. When Democratic presidential candidate William Jennings Bryan called for immediate independence in the Philippines, Taft was alarmed. He believed this encouraged revolutionaries who still opposed American control.

Taft during his term as civil governor of the Philippines

After McKinley was reelected in 1900, Taft devised a fairer tax system for Filipinos, established municipal governments, improved roads and harbors, and placed as many natives as possible in government positions. All these things solidified Filipino support for the commission. By spring of 1901, the last of the significant rebel leaders had surrendered. Governance of the islands was then turned over to a purely civil government, with a strong police force.

Taft was sworn in as the Philippines' first civil governor on July 4, 1901. By that time, he was confident of his ability to accomplish his goals there and had developed a deep commitment to the people. However, he was by that time significantly overweight. That excess weight, coupled with the tropical heat, fever, intestinal problems, and his relentless schedule, had seriously affected his health. He was also devastated by the assassination in September of President McKinley, who had always backed him in his many disputes with U.S. military personnel. By Thanksgiving of 1901, Taft had endured two surgeries, and on Christmas Eve he and his family sailed back to the United States so that he could recuperate.

Taft quickly found that he had the support and confidence of Theodore Roosevelt, who had become president upon McKinley's death. Before returning to the islands, he traveled to Rome, Italy, at Roosevelt's request to settle one of the Philippines' most troublesome problems. Over the years, Spanish missionaries known as friars had accumulated some 400,000 acres of prime land in the islands. By threatening the peasants with rejection by God, they had wrongfully acquired lands that should have belonged to the common people. These friars had come to be viewed as symbols of greed and of foreign domination. Ultimately, they drove the people into open revolt. In 1896, a rebel force led by Emilio Aguinaldo drove the friars from the islands and proclaimed their lands the property of the people. The rebels threatened to murder any friars who attempted to return to reclaim their lands.

Filipino rebels are executed in Manila in 1897.

However, the Treaty of Paris, which gave the United States control of the islands, guaranteed the friars' property rights. Both McKinley and Roosevelt agreed that this dispute was a civil, rather than religious, one. Yet settling it was a very delicate matter. No one wished to anger American Catholics or to provoke a dispute with Pope Leo XIII, who ruled the Roman Catholic church from Rome. After extensive negotiations, Taft persuaded the church to sell most of the land to the Philippine government. The land was then gradually parceled out to the natives on generous terms.

When Taft returned to the islands, he had to cope with further problems: cholera, famine, bands of outlaws, and his own amoebic dysentery. Yet he was so committed to his

Elihu Root

mission there that he twice declined Roosevelt's offers of a
seat on the Supreme Court. Though that remained his
most cherished goal, he felt he could not yet leave the
Filipino people.

Despite his ill health and his weight of about three
hundred pounds, Taft traveled twenty-five miles on
horseback through mountainous country on one of his
goodwill missions. After the trip, he cabled to Elihu Root:
"Stood trip well. Rode horseback twenty-five miles to five
thousand feet elevation." Root immediately replied: "How
is the horse?" Such was Taft's jovial nature that he
delighted in this story and passed it on to reporters.

Chapter 5

Troubleshooting as Secretary of War

When Theodore Roosevelt began his first full term as president in 1905, he once again asked Taft to return to Washington. This time, he urged Taft to assume the post of secretary of war, which Elihu Root had resigned. As usual, Taft consulted his family, who strongly supported the move. Charles again stepped in to help: when he learned that William was afraid he could not live as a cabinet member on the $8,000-a-year salary, he immediately offered a $6,000-per-year supplement. Two other considerations convinced Taft to accept the position. First, as secretary of war, he would have administrative responsibility for the Philippines. Thus, he could maintain his influence in the islands. Second, he was doubtful that his amoebic dysentery would be cured if he remained in the tropics. He took office on February 1, 1905, and soon became Roosevelt's principal mediator and problem solver throughout the world.

One of his first jobs was to oversee the construction of the Panama Canal in Central America. By the time Taft became secretary of war, Roosevelt had acquired the land needed for the canal's construction. The work of designing and building it had been delegated to a commission, but many problems remained. The Panamanians, for instance, feared that Americans would dominate Panama. Roosevelt sent Taft to reassure them.

While he was in Panama, Taft backed up Dr. William C. Gorgas, the chief sanitary officer of the canal commission. Gorgas insisted that the yellow fever plaguing the workers could be controlled only by destroying the mosquitoes that were spreading it. This does not seem very remarkable today, but at the time, most people considered Gorgas's theory that mosquitoes spread yellow fever to be ridiculous.

Taft also recommended Major George W. Goethals as chief engineer of the project. The first two men who had held that position had walked off the job in frustration over indecision and delays. Goethals, however, stayed with the project and made the canal a reality.

As secretary of war, Taft also helped negotiate a growing territorial dispute between Japan and Russia. Meeting with the Japanese premier, he concluded a secret agreement under which the United States would support Japan's claim to Korea.

In 1907, he was sent again to Japan to deal with alarm over anti-Japanese sentiment in California. At one point, San Francisco school authorities were excluding children of Japanese descent from classes. Though Roosevelt quickly protested and the policy was retracted, tensions remained high. In Japan, Taft met with both the Japanese foreign minister and the emperor to reassure them of America's desire to preserve peace. The Japanese leaders, in turn, assured Taft that Japan had no designs on the Philippines, which had been one of Roosevelt's concerns.

Taft also calmed a potentially explosive situation in Cuba as secretary of war. The treaty that ended the Spanish-American War supposedly had granted independence to Cuba. However, the island was in fact entirely dependent upon America for its defense and its economy. America dominated the government of Cuban president Thomas Estrada Palma, and by 1906, rebel resistance to that government was reaching a crisis. Taft arranged to have troops ready in case quick intervention became necessary.

In the late summer of that year, Roosevelt was alarmed enough to call Taft back from a family vacation in Murray Bay and send him personally to Cuba. Once there, Taft found that Palma had lost control of most of the country; afraid for his own safety, he was eager to resign and turn the government over to the United States. In spite of Taft's persuasions, Palma resigned, and Taft himself had to step in as provisional governor for a few weeks. He was careful, however, to act always as if Cuba were an independent republic. Eventually he succeeded in getting most of the rebels to turn in their arms. In October, he turned the governorship over to Charles E. Magoon. By January of 1909, America was able to withdraw its troops from the island.

Above: The Panama Canal commission: Goethals (center) and Gorgas (next to last)
Below: Taft and one of his brothers (left, seated) at the Panama Canal

Above: Taft having his picture taken with Japanese dignitaries in Tokyo

Right: Cuban president Thomas Estrada Palma

Chapter 6

Embarking on a Nightmare

For most of his adult life, Taft had campaigned for Republican candidates. He detested the process, however, and commented after campaigning hard for Roosevelt's 1904 election, "A national campaign for the presidency is to me a nightmare." Yet the pressures on him to run for president in 1908 were mounting. Nellie desperately wanted him to pursue the nomination, as did most of the rest of the family. Roosevelt had vowed not to seek another term. Instead, he encouraged Taft to seek the office.

Meanwhile, William Jennings Bryan, the expected Democratic nominee, was calling for public ownership of the railroads. Taft viewed this as socialism. He saw Bryan as an anarchist, that is, one who has totally rejected the established order. Alarmed by what he considered Bryan's radicalism, Taft believed it his patriotic duty to ensure a Republican victory. He preferred to back another candidate, particularly Roosevelt or Elihu Root. However, once it became apparent that neither of them would run, he reluctantly agreed to become a candidate.

By 1908, Taft was fifty-one years old, with over twenty-five years of successful public service behind him. Nevertheless, he lacked the inner confidence of an effective leader. He easily won the Republican nomination but let Roosevelt dominate the campaign. In fact, he deferred so often to Roosevelt that it became a campaign joke: "T.A.F.T." means "Take Advice from Theodore." Nellie, who had never trusted Roosevelt, agonized over the fact that his applause at the convention lasted longer than Taft's. She was resentful of his constant meddling in the campaign, but Taft welcomed it and looked constantly to Roosevelt for support and approval. In speech after speech, he assured voters that he was committed to Roosevelt's principles. Often he mentioned Roosevelt's opposition to the concentration of wealth in too few hands.

Though Taft was nervous throughout the campaign, it was not really a close race. William Jennings Bryan, the Democratic candidate, had run twice before. His calls for public ownership of the railroads and for free coinage of silver had caused many people to view him as radical. Though he had moderated his positions to some extent by 1908, he still frightened business interests. Also, despite Taft's unpopularity with labor unions, Bryan never managed to develop strong union support.

Taft's religion was a minor issue in the campaign. Like his father, he was a Unitarian. That meant that he believed in God but did not accept the divinity of Christ. In 1889, he had cited his religion as one of his reasons for turning down an invitation to seek the presidency of Yale. He felt that Yale's conservative graduates would be shocked by his

A jovial Taft chats on the telephone.

beliefs. In 1908, some of his critics attacked him as an "infidel" unfit to run the country. Others had mistakenly concluded that he was a Roman Catholic because of his negotiations with the pope during the Philippine controversy; they attacked him as a slave to the pope. Taft refused to be bothered by the controversy, stating to one supporter, "If the American electorate is so narrow as not to elect a Unitarian, well and good. I can stand it."

Election day brought an easy victory for Taft and his running mate, James S. Sherman. They drew over a million more popular votes than the Democrats and won the electoral vote 321 to 162. Taft, who had waited for the returns at his brother's home in Cincinnati, assured a group of well-wishers that his administration would be "a worthy successor to that of Theodore Roosevelt."

Chapter 7

A Fish Out of Water

When Taft awoke on his inauguration day, March 4, 1909, he found the trees and streets of Washington, D.C., coated with ice from a blizzard the night before. It was a fitting omen for a man who had commented, even after his election, that he felt "like a fish out of water" in taking on the burdens of the presidency. Taft's family and friends often had been right in assuring him that he could handle an assignment that he feared. No one can blame them for urging him on to this high office. But his mother had been right when she had warned him that politics would make him miserable.

Taft was ill-suited for the presidency. He set back, rather than advanced, some of his most cherished projects, and suffered personal humiliation when his reelection bid was soundly rejected by the American people.

Simply being in office after Roosevelt posed a problem for Taft, since people naturally compared the two. Roosevelt was a master of the dramatic gesture. His sweeping phrases charmed the public, while covering up his general disregard for structure and detail.

Opposite page: Campaigning for president 45

Taft, on the other hand, was a private, careful, and painfully honest man. He was also unremittingly conservative and slavishly devoted to living within the law. As president, he did much to convert Roosevelt's grand policies into actual achievements. But because he was unable to make the big boast and to sweep aside the rules, many Americans believed he was retreating from Roosevelt's daring ideas.

Thus, he lost the support not only of Roosevelt himself, but also of those who admired his brash predecessor. At the same time, his *actual* success in carrying out Roosevelt's ideas hurt his popularity with those who had *opposed* Roosevelt.

Taft also lacked Roosevelt's remarkable skill in manipulating the press. He was intensely uncomfortable with reporters and generally would not speak with them at all. Consequently, they rarely heard his side of the story. He never hired anyone to handle his relations with the press. Neither did he employ Roosevelt's very useful device of leaking ideas to the press in order to test their popularity before he actually carried them out.

He also vastly overestimated the sophistication of the average citizen. Over and over again, he wrongly assumed that he need not respond to misguided attacks. He assumed such charges would be seen as baseless propaganda. He selected a cabinet full of corporate lawyers, thinking that those who had worked for the major corporations would be best at developing ways to restrain them. He was immediately attacked for allowing his cabinet to be ruled by the same industrial types he had pledged to fight.

Though he wrote eloquently to friends about his true motives, he never made those motives clear to the public.

Taft's insecurity led him to seek the advice and support of some leaders in Congress who were seen as enemies of Roosevelt and all he stood for. Most notable of these were Speaker of the House Joseph G. Cannon and Senator Nelson W. Aldrich. Cannon was a corrupt leader who ruled the House through favoritism and fear. Aldrich was a champion of the high tariffs that both Taft and Roosevelt opposed and was a major ally of industrial trusts.

Baffled by being misunderstood, and insecure about his ability to govern, Taft became less and less willing to make decisions. His lifelong tendency to put things off reached serious proportions, and he frequently lost battles simply by failing to act at the proper moment.

All these professional troubles had already alarmed Taft to the point of misery, when he suffered a personal disaster as well. In May of 1909, his cherished Nellie collapsed on the presidential yacht; she could not speak when she was roused. Apparently a small blood vessel in her brain had burst. Though the effects were not great, she developed speech problems and fled Washington for the family's summer cottage at Beverly, Massachusetts. Thus, Taft was deprived of his most valued counselor and supporter at a time when he was most weighed down by the burdens of office.

By the end of June of his first year in the presidency, Taft was overwhelmed by the hopelessness of his task. He confided to his brother that he doubted he would have a second term.

Left: Taft and Roosevelt
in front of the White House
before leaving for the
Capitol on Taft's snowy
inauguration day

Below: Taft reviews the parade
after his inauguration.
A fierce blizzard, with flashes
of lightning, rain, snow, and a
cutting wind, made it one of the
roughest inauguration days ever.

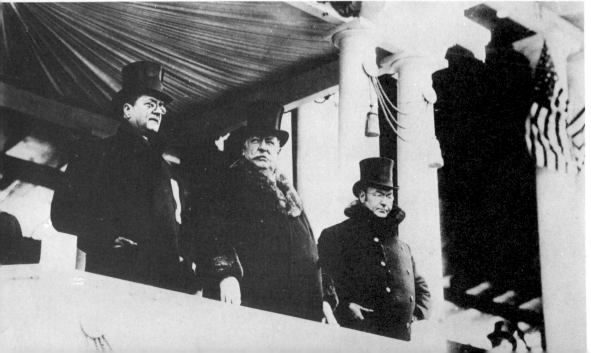

Right: The First Lady

Below: President and Mrs. Taft in the inaugural parade

Above: Taft with his brother Charles
Below: Taft with golfing buddies

Above: Taft and family during the first year of his presidency
Below: The Tafts' cottage in Beverly, Massachusetts

Chapter 8

Where Angels Dare Not Tread

Some political battles are so controversial that most presidents avoid them. Taft was either too committed or simply too naive to stay out of some such battles. The most obvious of these was his campaign for tariff revision. A tariff is a tax on imported goods. Countries impose tariffs to protect goods produced at home. A tariff raises the price of imported products, so that buyers will prefer to purchase lower-priced domestic goods.

However, tariffs are a tricky business. President Grover Cleveland had recognized the dangers but plunged head-long into a fight to lower tariffs in 1887. When his advisers attempted to restrain him, he responded, "What is the use of being elected or re-elected unless you stand for something?" It was a noble sentiment, but politically dangerous. Cleveland did succeed in bringing down the tariff rates. This made imported goods cheaper, which pleased consumers but angered American manufacturers. They became so hostile that they threatened wage slashes and even layoffs if Cleveland were reelected. After losing the election in 1888, he told a friend, "I don't regret it. It is better to be defeated battling for an honest principle than to win by a cowardly subterfuge."

Roosevelt had had no such romantic notions. Though he initially supported lowering tariffs, his advisers convinced him to back off. Taft, however, felt bound to pursue the issue.

Tariff rates were at their highest point in the nation's history. The Republican party platform in 1908 had come out clearly in favor of tariff reform, and Taft had campaigned for modest changes in tariff rates. Now as president, he plunged ahead with attempts to secure the promised revisions.

Taft called a special session of Congress in 1909 to deal with tariffs. Although it had been clear at the Republican convention that "tariff revision" had meant tariff *reduction*, Taft sent no clear message to Congress regarding the nature of the changes to be made. Powerful Republicans who favored *high* tariffs claimed that the party had promised simply a restructuring of tariffs to ensure that all were fair — not a general reduction. When Taft failed to dispute this or to insist on reductions, he was quickly attacked by those who favored lower rates.

In April, the House passed the Payne bill, which contained modest reductions. In the Senate, however, the bill was rewritten drastically. The principal sponsor there was the conservative Aldrich, who claimed the party had not promised to *reduce* tariffs. Taft could and probably should have attacked Aldrich and his allies for having rejected their own party's platform. He failed to do so for a number of reasons. One was simply that he detested political conflict. Another was that he was insecure about his relations with Congress and had already come to depend upon

Aldrich for advice and support. Yet another reason was that those who most strongly demanded reductions were men he considered radicals and demagogues; he did not wish to be associated with them. Thus, he secretly worked against Aldrich and his allies but made no public attack on them. He threatened to veto the bill if it failed to conform to the Republican platform.

A joint committee of the House and Senate debated into the summer over the Payne-Aldrich bill. Those who wanted high tariffs pointed to the national debt, since tariffs were a major source of the federal government's income at the time. Those who favored a reduction threatened to pass an income tax to make up the shortage. Taft was against this idea, since the Supreme Court had declared an income tax unconstitutional. He thought Congress should not flaunt the court's rulings.

Speaker Cannon then threatened to adjourn the House of Representatives without taking action on the tariff bill. Taft, in a rare moment of courage, promised to call another special session immediately if Cannon carried out his threat.

Ultimately, the committee yielded to Taft's demands and produced a compromise bill. The bill included lower tariffs on the most important items but higher tariffs on others. It also included a corporate income tax and a proposal to amend the Constitution so that an individual income tax could be imposed. Taft agreed to support the compromise; he was eager to avoid the extreme demands of either of the warring factions. He signed the bill on August 5, 1909.

Taft meeting with his cabinet members in 1912

Commentators immediately attacked the bill as a betrayal of the Republican platform. They exaggerated the tariff increases and called the reductions insignificant. Taft asserted in a speech that it was "the best bill the Republican party has ever passed." The newspapers took his statement to mean that he wholeheartedly supported the compromise. Actually, Taft was simply stating what was accurate: that the Payne-Aldrich Act was the first downward revision of tariff rates ever passed by a Republican Congress. But the frenzied attack by the newspapers totally obscured Taft's meaning. The hostility of the newspapers may have been fueled by self-interest: publishers had passionately but unsuccessfully pushed for an elimination of the import tax on print paper.

Above: A cartoon showing Lady Liberty and Uncle Sam toasting Taft, who promises to serve up a platter of peace and prosperity

Right: A quote from Abraham Lincoln, which Taft held as his Presidential motto

" IF I were to try to read, much less answer, all the attacks made on me, this shop might as well be closed for any other business. I do the very best I know how—the very best I can; and I mean to keep on doing so until the end. If the end brings me out all right, what is said against me won't amount to anything. If the end brings me out wrong, ten angels swearing I was right would make no difference.' "

"Speeches and Presidential addresses" by Abraham Lincoln

Roosevelt's lax policies led to Louis Glavis's attack on Richard Ballinger.
Taft, caught in the middle of this embarrassing situation, tries to calm things down.

Chapter 9

The Ballinger-Pinchot Affair

At the time of Taft's election, the United States still owned a vast amount of undeveloped land that could be claimed by homesteaders who came in to settle it. The federal government was allowed to hold back certain lands, including those that might be valuable sources of water power or minerals. Roosevelt and his secretary of the interior were eager to conserve open space and national resources. With that goal in mind, they had withheld thousands of acres from homesteading. (In many cases, there was very little evidence that these lands were actually valuable energy sources.) They had been enthusiastically supported in that effort by Gifford Pinchot, the head of the United States Forest Service.

The arrival of Taft and his secretary of the interior, Richard A. Ballinger, was a dark day for Pinchot. He had become accustomed to Roosevelt's freewheeling ways and contempt for rules. Now he had to deal with Ballinger's insistence that lands be withheld strictly in accordance with the law. Hostile to Ballinger already, Pinchot was easily convinced when an agent of the Interior Department, Louis R. Glavis, accused Ballinger of wrongdoing.

The Interior Department's Louis R. Glavis

Glavis claimed that Ballinger was involved in a conspiracy to allow a private oil company to acquire thousands of acres of valuable public land. Taft spent several days evaluating these accusations and reviewing Glavis's files. Later historians have concluded there was little, if any, evidence of wrongdoing. In fact, the lands in dispute were not actually rich in coal, as Glavis asserted. Taft concluded not only that Glavis was wrong but also that he had deliberately concealed information that showed Ballinger's innocence. Taft was outraged by what he viewed as a cheap and baseless attack on one of his own cabinet members; he made strong public statements of his confidence in Ballinger and supported Ballinger's decision to fire Glavis.

Glavis then took his story to the popular magazine *Collier's Weekly*. *Collier's* ran it without checking its accuracy.

Gifford Pinchot, head of the U.S. Forest Service

Roosevelt would have responded to this type of attack on a cabinet member by calling in the press and soundly denouncing the allegations and the men who made them. But Taft was simply incapable of that kind of tirade. He continued to support Ballinger, though he did so in ponderous statements about his careful review of the evidence, rather than in flamboyant attacks on the "enemy."

Taft suspected that Gifford Pinchot was trying to provoke Taft into firing him. He tried hard to avoid a fight with Pinchot, knowing that any conflict between them would be seen as a break with Roosevelt and a rejection of conservationism. In 1910, however, Pinchot wrote to a congressman affirming his belief in Glavis's charges. The letter was made public, and that left Taft little choice. After consulting with Elihu Root, he fired Pinchot.

Cartoon captioned "Spare the rod and spoil the conservation policy"

Ballinger demanded a congressional investigation into the charges. That investigation, which ran from January to May of 1910, produced no evidence of any wrongdoing by Ballinger. It did, however, result in a modest embarrassment to the scrupulously honest president. Fearful of libel charges, *Collier's* hired Louis Brandeis, a brilliant attorney who would one day sit on the Supreme Court with Taft, to represent Glavis. One of the key documents in the case was a memorandum to Taft summarizing the evidence against Ballinger. The memorandum was dated *prior* to Taft's statement that he found no evidence of Ballinger's wrongdoing. However, Brandeis found that it had actually

The accused, Secretary of the Interior Richard A. Ballinger

been prepared *after* Taft's statement. This created the false impression that Taft had not actually based his decision on a thorough review of the evidence. The incident long proved a thorn in Taft's side; when he eventually became chief justice, it delayed his acceptance of Brandeis as a respected colleague on the court.

Throughout this ordeal, Taft rejected Ballinger's offers to resign. He finally yielded in March of 1911, when Ballinger decided to leave because of poor health and economic concerns. In a touching farewell letter, he said that Ballinger had suffered terribly and unfairly at the hands of hypocrites who conspired against him.

Chapter 10

What the President Did

Though abused by writers in his own time as a great failure, Taft was not really so unsuccessful a president as he was painted. He was completely unable to lead or to shape public opinion. In addition, the presidency brought out his worst traits: indecisiveness, procrastination, and irritability. Yet he had real gifts: a fine judicial mind, a sense of fair play, and great skill as a mediator. Those gifts enabled him to make progress on issues he considered important.

As a trust buster, he was actually more successful than Roosevelt. Taft had been highly criticized for selecting George W. Wickersham, a corporate lawyer, as attorney general. But Wickersham rapidly set himself apart from his old pals. He followed through vigorously on prosecutions begun under Roosevelt's administration and initiated many more under Taft.

Though he was viewed as an enemy of organized labor, Taft did obtain some modest benefits for working people. He established the Bureau of Mines to cut down on what he called "the awful losses of life in the operation of mines."

He also secured safety laws and workers' compensation for railroad employees. He established a bureau to deal with the problems of child laborers, and to head it he appointed Julia Lathrop, the first woman ever to head a federal government bureau. Though unsuccessful, he made a sincere attempt to have Congress prohibit the stopping of labor strikes. However, he did veto a labor-supported bill that would have required immigrants to be able to read in order to be admitted to the United States.

Taft also instituted a postal savings bank plan, which Roosevelt had supported but had done little to promote. Small and isolated investors could deposit their money in postal savings banks without fear of losing it to unstable banks. The United States was, at the turn of the century, one of the few civilized nations that did *not* have such a system. Taft pushed Congress to pass the bill, and he signed it on June 25, 1910. Thus he had accomplished what eight postmasters general, over the preceding forty years, had been unable to do.

Taft also pushed Congress to create a Commerce Court to resolve legal problems over railroad rates. He increased the powers of the Interstate Commerce Commission as well, and secured for the commission the power to supervise telephone and telegraph lines.

Through the Tariff Board, he began the first scientific investigation of tariff rates. He made the first serious attempt to prepare and implement a federal budget. He resisted the temptation to use his hiring power as a political weapon, and he oversaw the admission of New Mexico and Arizona as states.

The projects Taft promoted unsuccessfully may tell us more about him than those in which he succeeded. His willingness to tackle the thorny issue of tariffs has already been discussed. He also worked doggedly for free trade between Canada and the United States. This was opposed by American farmers and feared by Canadians. They believed that Americans would use a free-trade policy to dominate Canada.

Undaunted, Taft campaigned relentlessly, even meeting personally with the National Grange, an alliance of farmers, to plead his case. He hounded Congress; he argued openly with the lumber and paper manufacturers, who feared Canadian competition; and he ultimately convinced Congress to approve a dramatic increase in "free" items and a reduction in the rates on many more. To his great disappointment, however, the Canadian people rejected the plan.

Taft had great faith in courts and a marked distaste for conflict. That drove him to seek a way to resolve international disputes without war. He acted as honorary president of the new American Society for the Judicial Settlement of International Disputes. He publicly called for submitting all international disputes to arbitration. Stating his position simply, he commented, "If we do not have arbitration, we shall have war."

He nursed through Congress a joint resolution calling for the use of international agencies to promote arms control and to develop a worldwide peacekeeping navy. Unfortunately, European response to these suggestions was lukewarm, and the effort petered out.

**Children once formed one-third of the industrial labor force in the United States.
Above: A girl at a spinning machine.   Below: Boys working in a factory at midnight**

Right: Children working as miners in Pennsylvania

Below: A young boy at work in a glass factory

Left: An Italian immigrant
family at Ellis Island
in New York City, 1905

Below: The Great Hall at
Ellis Island in 1911, where
thousands of immigrants
were processed for admission
to the United States

The signing of the arbitration treaty between England, France, and the United States. Seated are British ambassador James Bryce (left) and U.S. Secretary of State P. C. Knox.

Taft pushed on in his drive to make war a thing of the past. He eventually reached an agreement with Great Britain and France to submit certain international disputes to arbitration. Unable to convince the Senate to approve this agreement, he took his case to the people. He traveled throughout the West in the fall of 1911 to drum up support for the treaties. His confidence that the American people would rally to the cause of world peace was sadly misplaced. No swell of popular support emerged, and the Senate altered the treaties beyond recognition. Taft never even presented them to Great Britain and France.

Many years later, looking back on this incident, he commented: "So I put [the treaties] on the shelf and let the dust accumulate on them in the hope that the senators might change their minds, or that the people might change the Senate; instead of which they changed me."

Chapter 11

The Split with Roosevelt
and the 1912 Campaign

Since his years in the Philippines, Taft had been enchanted with Theodore Roosevelt. Roosevelt was a dashing war hero who detested rules. His casual self-assurance was the opposite of Taft's careful, conservative approach. Perhaps Taft admired the ease with which Roosevelt seemed to meet all challenges. In agreeing to run for president at all, he had depended heavily on Roosevelt's encouragement. Roosevelt, in turn, had great confidence in Taft in those days. He assigned Taft, as his secretary of war, to extremely delicate negotiations. He pushed Taft to run for the presidency, and he exulted, when advised of Taft's nomination, "I do not believe there can be found in the whole country a man so well fitted to be President."

Roosevelt departed on an African safari immediately after Taft's inauguration. He was apparently trying to distance himself from American politics and to avoid appearing to dominate the new president. Unfortunately for Taft, Roosevelt, and the Republican party, it was not that simple. Roosevelt had expected Taft to remain a genial underling, a perfect disciple. Instead, it rapidly began to appear that Taft was changing course. Roosevelt became more and more alarmed at Taft's performance, and Taft, in turn, worried constantly about Roosevelt's approval. He was well aware that his political enemies were flooding Roosevelt with rumors. Taft dreaded facing Roosevelt when he returned from Africa. If the two had been able to communicate regularly and with their old confidence, Roosevelt might have built up Taft's political courage, and Taft might have softened some of Roosevelt's more radical views. But that was not to be.

After Roosevelt's return to the country, they continued to communicate only through rumor and guarded correspondence. Roosevelt began to meet openly with those who were viewed as Taft's enemies. It became apparent to Taft that Roosevelt's opinion was more highly valued than his. What was worse, those who met with Roosevelt began to speak of him as the only one who could set the Republican party back on the right path in 1912.

Roosevelt's public pronouncements became more and more radical, and Taft responded by retreating further into conservatism. Roosevelt began to question the concept of states' rights (that is, the idea that the states retain all rights that the Constitution does not specifically delegate to the federal government). Taft concluded that Roosevelt was out to destroy the Constitution. Roosevelt also called for citizens' rights to throw judges out of office and to overturn judges' decisions. These positions horrified Taft.

Miserable in the presidency, Taft had no desire for a second term. Yet he began to see himself as the only one who could stop his old friend from returning to power and

Taft and Wilson at Wilson's 1913 inauguration

imposing his radical notions on the country. He wrote to his brother Horace that he felt compelled to stay in the race as "the only hope against radicalism and demagogy." (Demagogy is the use of popular prejudices and false claims to secure power.)

Taft, supported by the old guard of the party, easily won the Republican nomination. Roosevelt and his supporters then formed their own party. This split the Republican vote, and the three-way race ensured the election of the Democratic nominee, Woodrow Wilson. Taft trailed Roosevelt by almost a million popular votes, and won only Utah and Vermont. In consoling a friend who was heartsick at his loss, Taft wrote: "There was nothing done which cannot be recalled and which will not be promptly recalled when the time comes, and in the end we shall see that popular government is the most enduring and the most just and the most effective."

Chapter 12

After the Fall

Almost the moment he realized he would no longer be president, Taft regained his usual good spirits and charm. His mood was lifted even more when, shortly after the election, he was offered a professorship at Yale. Though he regretted being unable to return to Cincinnati, he was relieved to be spared the problems of practicing law once again.

The popularity that he had enjoyed before the presidency also returned as people learned of his good sportsmanship and genuine good wishes for Wilson. He spoke widely during the eight years he spent at Yale and wrote extensively for publication. The considerable income he received from these activities supplemented his $5,000 annual salary as a professor. By now, Nellie's speech had returned to normal; the children were all out of the house and were doing well. Robert was studying law at Harvard, Charles was attending the preparatory school run by Horace Taft, and Helen was at Bryn Mawr College.

**Opposite page: Taft in his
Yale University academic robes**

Though there is no evidence that Taft ever hoped or expected to return to the presidency, he remained politically active and involved in civic affairs. At Wilson's request, he served as president of the commission that erected the Lincoln Memorial in Washington, D.C. Like Wilson, he hoped America could avoid the conflict in Europe that eventually became World War I. However, he vigorously supported the war effort once the United States entered it. He promoted Liberty Loans to finance the war effort and gave inspirational speeches to draftees. He also served, at Wilson's request, on the War Labor Board—a commitment that required him to abandon teaching for a time and relocate in Washington, D.C.

It was his service on the War Labor Board that brought him, for the first time in his life, into direct contact with the day-to-day problems of workers. He astonished labor leaders with his liberal decisions. One of the board's principles, for instance, was the relatively radical idea of a "living wage." That is, the board attempted to set the minimum wage at the level it took "to insure the subsistence of the worker and his family in health and reasonable comfort." Taft was unwavering in his commitment to the living wage. He even sided with labor on the question of whether low wages could be justified by a company's poor financial condition. Taft said that they could not, and he compared the purchase of labor to that of any other commodity. He noted that no one would require the supplier of any other material to sell his wares at a lower price, just because the buyer could not afford the going rate.

It was also on the War Labor Board that Taft, for the first time in his life, stretched the law a bit to achieve what he considered a just result. Some employers were requiring their employees to sign "yellow dog" contracts. These contracts made the employees agree not to join labor unions in order to get work. Earlier Supreme Court decisions suggested that the board could not prohibit such contracts; yet the War Labor Board, with Taft's support, voted to ban them.

Taft also continued his efforts to create some means of resolving disputes between nations. In 1915, he accepted the presidency of the League to Enforce Peace. This organization favored an international court to arbitrate disputes and advise peaceful solutions. Members would agree to resist any war begun by a member *without* arbitration.

Though President Wilson was also promoting the idea of an international agreement to avoid future wars, he never really backed the League to Enforce Peace. Instead, he promoted his own concept, the League of Nations. He attempted to include the League in the peace treaty that ended World War I. Taft asked his fellow Republicans to set aside their hostility to Wilson and support the League of Nations. He said that it did not matter who got the credit, so long as the League came into existence. But resistance was too strong, especially from those who feared that the pact would draw the United States into a foreign war it did not want to fight. The Senate rejected the proposed treaty, and the United States never joined the League of Nations.

Chapter 13

A Lifelong Dream Fulfilled

When Edward White, chief justice of the Supreme Court, died in 1921, Taft's hopes soared. Warren Harding, who was president, had promised him the post. Harding proposed Taft's name on June 30, 1921, and the appointment was confirmed the same day. Taft was ecstatic at the fulfillment of his life's dream; he reveled in the congratulations that poured in. He felt that the nation had paid him back after his humiliating defeat in 1912.

As chief justice, he worked incessantly; he rose at 5:15 A.M. in order to devote two hours to the court's work before breakfast. He returned to his study in the evening after dinner. Virtually his only "time off" was an hour for dinner and the hour he took to walk the three miles from his home on Wyoming Avenue to the Capitol. The pace he maintained was suited to the task he faced: when he came on the bench, there were 343 cases waiting for decisions; 421 more had been filed by the following February. He pushed himself mercilessly and agonized over the slowness of his eight associate justices. He realized from the start, however, that the problem could not be resolved simply by encouraging them to work harder.

To deal with the backlog of cases, Taft took a number of significant steps. When one or more justices disagreed, one of them had to spend time writing a "dissenting" opinion. So to save time, Taft pushed the other justices hard to make unanimous decisions. He proposed and successfully pushed through Congress the creation of a Conference of Senior Circuit Court Judges, with the chief justice at its head. This conference attempted to assign judges according to work load and to improve procedures of the federal courts. Though it had fairly limited powers, the conference became a significant force in succeeding years. Taft argued that the judicial system had to be streamlined. He said that equal justice under the law depended upon the swift processing of cases, since "[a] rich man can stand the delay and profits by it, but the poor man always suffers."

No amount of coordination, however, could resolve the principal problem confronting the Supreme Court: it was floundering in a sea of insignificant cases. At the time Taft took office, for instance, the Supreme Court was required to hear any appeal from a lower federal court in which a party claimed that the Constitution was involved. Breaking with court tradition, Taft actively pressured Congress to allow the court to control its own work load. After three years, he finally got Congress to pass legislation that granted such control. From that point on, most cases could get heard in the Supreme Court only when the court agreed to hear them.

As chief justice, Taft is best remembered for these reforms and for his central role in getting a separate build-

Chief Justice and Mrs. Taft in the library of their Washington home

ing erected for the Supreme Court. His judicial decisions
are not particularly noteworthy. He was, however, a significant influence in several areas. A constitutional
amendment allowing personal income tax had passed since
Taft's years as president. Most of the challenges to the new
tax reached the Supreme Court during his term, and most
were rejected—even though the privileged wailed that this
redistribution of wealth was but thinly disguised socialism.

The Taft court was also called upon to decide most of the Prohibition cases. These were cases that arose out of the passage of the Eighteenth Amendment in 1919, which prohibited alcoholic beverages. Taft had considered Prohibition a dreadful idea, unenforceable and bound to provoke lawlessness. Once he was on the bench, however, he enforced it strictly. For instance, he ruled that Britain could not ship liquor from Canada to Mexico by way of the United States, even though a U.S.-British treaty allowed this. He also upheld the ruling that a person could be prosecuted under both state and federal law for possession of the same liquor, even though this constituted two prosecutions for the same crime.

In labor cases, he was guided by two fundamental principles. The first was that labor had a perfect right to organize, to bargain collectively, and to strike. The second principle was that labor should enjoy no special privileges in connection with these actions. Thus, in the case entitled *American Steel Foundries vs. Tri-City Central Trades Council*, he restricted union picketing because it had gone beyond persuasion and into intimidation. In *Truax vs. Corrigan*, he overturned an Arizona law that was supportive of strikes. Taft noted that other groups—such as competing businesses—would not have been allowed the type of conduct tolerated where unions were concerned. That, he said, was a failure to provide equal protection under the law, as mandated by the Fourteenth Amendment to the Constitution. In *United Mine Workers vs. Coronado Coal Company*, he ruled that companies could sue labor unions for damages.

On the other hand, he wrote one of his rare dissenting opinions in *Adkins vs. Children's Hospital*, which declared a minimum wage law unconstitutional. The majority of the justices thought that employees should work at any rate to which they had agreed. In his dissent, Taft argued that employees could not agree to work for less than minimum wage because the employer and the employees did not have equal bargaining power.

Despite the work load, Taft was never happier than during his term on the court. In 1923, he wrote, "The court . . . next to my wife and children, is the nearest thing to my heart in life."

Throughout his life, Taft's weight had soared when he was anxious and dropped when he was happy. It fell during his years on the court to 244 pounds—only a pound more than he had weighed upon graduation from Yale, some forty-five years earlier.

But the weight had taken its toll on his health. In 1922, he was hospitalized to have something described as "gravel" removed from his bladder. In the late winter of 1923, because of serious digestive disturbances, he had to miss President Wilson's funeral. That spring, he suffered from an internal inflammation. He began experiencing small heart attacks and admitted that he could not work as rapidly as he once could.

During his last years, Taft lived a secluded life in order to conserve his energy for his work on the court. When his brother Charles died in Cincinnati in 1929, however, Taft insisted on attending the funeral. Charles had loved and generously supported him all his life.

Taft attending commencement exercises at Yale in 1923

Taft returned to Washington so drained that his doctors advised him to take a break from his work. He grew weaker instead of stronger during his suggested retreat, and finally submitted his resignation to the president on February 3, 1930. After weeks of recognizing almost no one and being scarcely able to eat, he died at the age of seventy-two on March 8, 1930.

**Above: Chief Justice Taft swears in Herbert Hoover as president in 1929.
Below: Hoover and others attending Taft's burial in Arlington National Cemetery**

Above: Taft taking his oath as chief justice of the Supreme Court
Below: The Tafts with their children and grandchildren at Murray Bay

William Howard Taft, 1857-1930

Chronology of American History

(Shaded area covers events in William Howard Taft's lifetime.)

About A.D. 982—Eric the Red, born in Norway, reaches Greenland in one of the first European voyages to North America.

About 1000—Leif Ericson (Eric the Red's son) leads what is thought to be the first European expedition to mainland North America; Leif probably lands in Canada.

1492—Christopher Columbus, seeking a sea route from Spain to the Far East, discovers the New World.

1497—John Cabot reaches Canada in the first English voyage to North America.

1513—Ponce de Léon explores Florida in search of the fabled Fountain of Youth.

1519-1521—Hernando Cortés of Spain conquers Mexico.

1534—French explorers led by Jacques Cartier enter the Gulf of St. Lawrence in Canada.

1540—Spanish explorer Francisco Coronado begins exploring the American Southwest, seeking the riches of the mythical Seven Cities of Cibola.

1565—St. Augustine, Florida, the first permanent European town in what is now the United States, is founded by the Spanish.

1607—Jamestown, Virginia, is founded, the first permanent English town in the present-day U.S.

1608—Frenchman Samuel de Champlain founds the village of Quebec, Canada.

1609—Henry Hudson explores the eastern coast of present-day U.S. for the Netherlands; the Dutch then claim parts of New York, New Jersey, Delaware, and Connecticut and name the area New Netherland.

1619—The English colonies' first shipment of black slaves arrives in Jamestown.

1620—English Pilgrims found Massachusetts' first permanent town at Plymouth.

1621—Massachusetts Pilgrims and Indians hold the famous first Thanksgiving feast in colonial America.

1623—Colonization of New Hampshire is begun by the English.

1624—Colonization of present-day New York State is begun by the Dutch at Fort Orange (Albany).

1625—The Dutch start building New Amsterdam (now New York City).

1630—The town of Boston, Massachusetts, is founded by the English Puritans.

1633—Colonization of Connecticut is begun by the English.

1634—Colonization of Maryland is begun by the English.

1636—Harvard, the colonies' first college, is founded in Massachusetts. Rhode Island colonization begins when Englishman Roger Williams founds Providence.

1638—Delaware colonization begins as Swedes build Fort Christina at present-day Wilmington.

1640—Stephen Daye of Cambridge, Massachusetts prints *The Bay Psalm Book*, the first English-language book published in what is now the U.S.

1643—Swedish settlers begin colonizing Pennsylvania.

About 1650—North Carolina is colonized by Virginia settlers.

1660—New Jersey colonization is begun by the Dutch at present-day Jersey City.

1670—South Carolina colonization is begun by the English near Charleston.

1673—Jacques Marquette and Louis Jolliet explore the upper Mississippi River for France.

1682—Philadelphia, Pennsylvania, is settled. La Salle explores Mississippi River all the way to its mouth in Louisiana and claims the whole Mississippi Valley for France.

1693—College of William and Mary is founded in Williamsburg, Virginia.

1700—Colonial population is about 250,000.

1703—Benjamin Franklin is born in Boston.

1732—George Washington, first president of the U.S., is born in Westmoreland County, Virginia.

1733—James Oglethorpe founds Savannah, Georgia; Georgia is established as the thirteenth colony.

1735—John Adams, second president of the U.S., is born in Braintree, Massachusetts.

1737—William Byrd founds Richmond, Virginia.

1738—British troops are sent to Georgia over border dispute with Spain.

1739—Black insurrection takes place in South Carolina.

1740—English Parliament passes act allowing naturalization of immigrants to American colonies after seven-year residence.

1743—Thomas Jefferson is born in Albemarle County, Virginia. Benjamin Franklin retires at age thirty-seven to devote himself to scientific inquiries and public service.

1744—King George's War begins; France joins war effort against England.

1745—During King George's War, France raids settlements in Maine and New York.

1747—Classes begin at Princeton College in New Jersey.

1748—The Treaty of Aix-la-Chapelle concludes King George's War.

1749—Parliament legally recognizes slavery in colonies and the inauguration of the plantation system in the South. George Washington becomes the surveyor for Culpepper County in Virginia.

1750—Thomas Walker passes through and names Cumberland Gap on his way toward Kentucky region. Colonial population is about 1,200,000.

1751—James Madison, fourth president of the U.S., is born in Port Conway, Virginia. English Parliament passes Currency Act, banning New England colonies from issuing paper money. George Washington travels to Barbados.

1752—Pennsylvania Hospital, the first general hospital in the colonies, is founded in Philadelphia. Benjamin Franklin uses a kite in a thunderstorm to demonstrate that lightning is a form of electricity.

1753—George Washington delivers command that the French withdraw from the Ohio River Valley; French disregard the demand. Colonial population is about 1,328,000.

1754—French and Indian War begins (extends to Europe as the Seven Years' War). Washington surrenders at Fort Necessity.

1755—French and Indians ambush Braddock. Washington becomes commander of Virginia troops.

1756—England declares war on France.

1758—James Monroe, fifth president of the U.S., is born in Westmoreland County, Virginia.

1759—Cherokee Indian war begins in southern colonies; hostilities extend to 1761. George Washington marries Martha Dandridge Custis.

1760—George III becomes king of England. Colonial population is about 1,600,000.

1762—England declares war on Spain.

1763—Treaty of Paris concludes the French and Indian War and the Seven Years' War. England gains Canada and most other French lands east of the Mississippi River.

1764—British pass the Sugar Act to gain tax money from the colonists. The issue of taxation without representation is first introduced in Boston. John Adams marries Abigail Smith.

1765—Stamp Act goes into effect in the colonies. Business virtually stops as almost all colonists refuse to use the stamps.

1766—British repeal the Stamp Act.

1767—John Quincy Adams, sixth president of the U.S. and son of second president John Adams, is born in Braintree, Massachusetts. Andrew Jackson, seventh president of the U.S., is born in Waxhaw settlement, South Carolina.

1769—Daniel Boone sights the Kentucky Territory.

1770—In the Boston Massacre, British soldiers kill five colonists and injure six. Townshend Acts are repealed, thus eliminating all duties on imports to the colonies except tea.

1771—Benjamin Franklin begins his autobiography, a work that he will never complete. The North Carolina assembly passes the "Bloody Act," which makes rioters guilty of treason.

1772—Samuel Adams rouses colonists to consider British threats to self-government.

1773—English Parliament passes the Tea Act. Colonists dressed as Mohawk Indians board British tea ships and toss 342 casks of tea into the water in what becomes known as the Boston Tea Party. William Henry Harrison is born in Charles City County, Virginia.

1774—British close the port of Boston to punish the city for the Boston Tea Party. First Continental Congress convenes in Philadelphia.

1775—American Revolution begins with battles of Lexington and Concord, Massachusetts. Second Continental Congress opens in Philadelphia. George Washington becomes commander-in-chief of the Continental army.

1776—Declaration of Independence is adopted on July 4.

1777—Congress adopts the American flag with thirteen stars and thirteen stripes. John Adams is sent to France to negotiate peace treaty.

1778—France declares war against Great Britain and becomes U.S. ally.

1779—British surrender to Americans at Vincennes. Thomas Jefferson is elected governor of Virginia. James Madison is elected to the Continental Congress.

1780—Benedict Arnold, first American traitor, defects to the British.

1781—Articles of Confederation go into effect. Cornwallis surrenders to George Washington at Yorktown, ending the American Revolution.

1782—American commissioners, including John Adams, sign peace treaty with British in Paris. Thomas Jefferson's wife, Martha, dies. Martin Van Buren is born in Kinderhook, New York.

1784—Zachary Taylor is born near Barboursville, Virginia.

1785—Congress adopts the dollar as the unit of currency. John Adams is made minister to Great Britain. Thomas Jefferson is appointed minister to France.

1786—Shays's Rebellion begins in Massachusetts.

1787—Constitutional Convention assembles in Philadelphia, with George Washington presiding; U.S. Constitution is adopted. Delaware, New Jersey, and Pennsylvania become states.

1788—Virginia, South Carolina, New York, Connecticut, New Hampshire, Maryland, and Massachusetts become states. U.S. Constitution is ratified. New York City is declared U.S. capital.

1789—Presidential electors elect George Washington and John Adams as first president and vice-president. Thomas Jefferson is appointed secretary of state. North Carolina becomes a state. French Revolution begins.

1790—Supreme Court meets for the first time. Rhode Island becomes a state. First national census in the U.S. counts 3,929,214 persons. John Tyler is born in Charles City County, Virginia.

1791—Vermont enters the Union. U.S. Bill of Rights, the first ten amendments to the Constitution, goes into effect. District of Columbia is established. James Buchanan is born in Stony Batter, Pennsylvania.

1792—Thomas Paine publishes *The Rights of Man*. Kentucky becomes a state. Two political parties are formed in the U.S., Federalist and Republican. Washington is elected to a second term, with Adams as vice-president.

1793—War between France and Britain begins; U.S. declares neutrality. Eli Whitney invents the cotton gin; cotton production and slave labor increase in the South.

1794—Eleventh Amendment to the Constitution is passed, limiting federal courts' power. "Whiskey Rebellion" in Pennsylvania protests federal whiskey tax. James Madison marries Dolley Payne Todd.

1795—George Washington signs the Jay Treaty with Great Britain. Treaty of San Lorenzo, between U.S. and Spain, settles Florida boundary and gives U.S. right to navigate the Mississippi. James Polk is born near Pineville, North Carolina.

1796—Tennessee enters the Union. Washington gives his Farewell Address, refusing a third presidential term. John Adams is elected president and Thomas Jefferson vice-president.

1797—Adams recommends defense measures against possible war with France. Napoleon Bonaparte and his army march against Austrians in Italy. U.S. population is about 4,900,000.

1798—Washington is named commander-in-chief of the U.S. Army. Department of the Navy is created. Alien and Sedition Acts are passed. Napoleon's troops invade Egypt and Switzerland.

1799—George Washington dies at Mount Vernon, New York. James Monroe is elected governor of Virginia. French Revolution ends. Napoleon becomes ruler of France.

1800—Thomas Jefferson and Aaron Burr tie for president. U.S. capital is moved from Philadelphia to Washington, D.C. The White House is built as presidents' home. Spain returns Louisiana to France. Millard Fillmore is born in Locke, New York.

1801—After thirty-six ballots, House of Representatives elects Thomas Jefferson president, making Burr vice-president. James Madison is named secretary of state.

1802—Congress abolishes excise taxes. U.S. Military Academy is founded at West Point, New York.

1803—Ohio enters the Union. Louisiana Purchase treaty is signed with France, greatly expanding U.S. territory.

1804—Twelfth Amendment to the Constitution rules that president and vice-president be elected separately. Alexander Hamilton is killed by Vice-President Aaron Burr in a duel. Orleans Territory is established. Napoleon crowns himself emperor of France. Franklin Pierce is born in Hillsborough Lower Village, New Hampshire.

1805—Thomas Jefferson begins his second term as president. Lewis and Clark expedition reaches the Pacific Ocean.

1806—Coinage of silver dollars is stopped; resumes in 1836.

1807—Aaron Burr is acquitted in treason trial. Embargo Act closes U.S. ports to trade.

1808—James Madison is elected president. Congress outlaws importing slaves from Africa. Andrew Johnson is born in Raleigh, North Carolina.

1809—Abraham Lincoln is born near Hodgenville, Kentucky.

1810—U.S. population is 7,240,000.

1811—William Henry Harrison defeats Indians at Tippecanoe. Monroe is named secretary of state.

1812—Louisiana becomes a state. U.S. declares war on Britain (War of 1812). James Madison is reelected president. Napoleon invades Russia.

1813—British forces take Fort Niagara and Buffalo, New York.

1814—Francis Scott Key writes "The Star-Spangled Banner." British troops burn much of Washington, D.C., including the White House. Treaty of Ghent ends War of 1812. James Monroe becomes secretary of war.

1815—Napoleon meets his final defeat at Battle of Waterloo.

1816—James Monroe is elected president. Indiana becomes a state.

1817—Mississippi becomes a state. Construction on Erie Canal begins.

1818—Illinois enters the Union. The present thirteen-stripe flag is adopted. Border between U.S. and Canada is agreed upon.

1819—Alabama becomes a state. U.S. purchases Florida from Spain. Thomas Jefferson establishes the University of Virginia.

1820—James Monroe is reelected. In the Missouri Compromise, Maine enters the Union as a free (non-slave) state.

1821—Missouri enters the Union as a slave state. Santa Fe Trail opens the American Southwest. Mexico declares independence from Spain. Napoleon Bonaparte dies.

1822—U.S. recognizes Mexico and Colombia. Liberia in Africa is founded as a home for freed slaves. Ulysses S. Grant is born in Point Pleasant, Ohio. Rutherford B. Hayes is born in Delaware, Ohio.

1823—Monroe Doctrine closes North and South America to European colonizing or invasion.

1824—House of Representatives elects John Quincy Adams president when none of the four candidates wins a majority in national election. Mexico becomes a republic.

1825—Erie Canal is opened. U.S. population is 11,300,000.

1826—Thomas Jefferson and John Adams both die on July 4, the fiftieth anniversary of the Declaration of Independence.

1828—Andrew Jackson is elected president. Tariff of Abominations is passed, cutting imports.

1829—James Madison attends Virginia's constitutional convention. Slavery is abolished in Mexico. Chester A. Arthur is born in Fairfield, Vermont.

1830—Indian Removal Act to resettle Indians west of the Mississippi is approved.

1831—James Monroe dies in New York City. James A. Garfield is born in Orange, Ohio. Cyrus McCormick develops his reaper.

1832—Andrew Jackson, nominated by the new Democratic Party, is reelected president.

1833—Britain abolishes slavery in its colonies. Benjamin Harrison is born in North Bend, Ohio.

1835—Federal government becomes debt-free for the first time.

1836—Martin Van Buren becomes president. Texas wins independence from Mexico. Arkansas joins the Union. James Madison dies at Montpelier, Virginia.

1837—Michigan enters the Union. U.S. population is 15,900,000. Grover Cleveland is born in Caldwell, New Jersey.

1840—William Henry Harrison is elected president.

1841—President Harrison dies in Washington, D.C., one month after inauguration. Vice-President John Tyler succeeds him.

1843—William McKinley is born in Niles, Ohio.

1844—James Knox Polk is elected president. Samuel Morse sends first telegraphic message.

1845—Texas and Florida become states. Potato famine in Ireland causes massive emigration from Ireland to U.S. Andrew Jackson dies near Nashville, Tennessee.

1846—Iowa enters the Union. War with Mexico begins.

1847—U.S. captures Mexico City.

1848—Zachary Taylor becomes president. Treaty of Guadalupe Hidalgo ends Mexico-U.S. war. Wisconsin becomes a state.

1849—James Polk dies in Nashville, Tennessee.

1850—President Taylor dies in Washington, D.C.; Vice-President Millard Fillmore succeeds him. California enters the Union, breaking tie between slave and free states.

1852—Franklin Pierce is elected president.

1853—Gadsen Purchase transfers Mexican territory to U.S.

1854—"War for Bleeding Kansas" is fought between slave and free states.

1855—Czar Nicholas I of Russia dies, succeeded by Alexander II.

1856—James Buchanan is elected president. In Massacre of Potawatomi Creek, Kansas-slavers are murdered by free-staters. Woodrow Wilson is born in Staunton, Pennsylvania.

1857—William Howard Taft is born in Cincinnati, Ohio.

1858—Minnesota enters the Union. Theodore Roosevelt is born in New York City.

1859—Oregon becomes a state.

1860—Abraham Lincoln is elected president; South Carolina secedes from the Union in protest.

1861—Arkansas, Tennessee, North Carolina, and Virginia secede. Kansas enters the Union as a free state. Civil War begins.

1862—Union forces capture Fort Henry, Roanoke Island, Fort Donelson, Jacksonville, and New Orleans; Union armies are defeated at the battles of Bull Run and Fredericksburg. Martin Van Buren dies in Kinderhook, New York. John Tyler dies near Charles City, Virginia.

1863—Lincoln issues Emancipation Proclamation: all slaves held in rebelling territories are declared free. West Virginia becomes a state.

1864—Abraham Lincoln is reelected. Nevada becomes a state.

1865—Lincoln is assassinated in Washington, D.C., and succeeded by Andrew Johnson. U.S. Civil War ends on May 26. Thirteenth Amendment abolishes slavery. Warren G. Harding is born in Blooming Grove, Ohio.

1867—Nebraska becomes a state. U.S. buys Alaska from Russia for $7,200,000. Reconstruction Acts are passed.

1868—President Johnson is impeached for violating Tenure of Office Act, but is acquitted by Senate. Ulysses S. Grant is elected president. Fourteenth Amendment prohibits voting discrimination. James Buchanan dies in Lancaster, Pennsylvania.

1869—Franklin Pierce dies in Concord, New Hampshire.

1870—Fifteenth Amendment gives blacks the right to vote.

1872—Grant is reelected over Horace Greeley. General Amnesty Act pardons ex-Confederates. Calvin Coolidge is born in Plymouth Notch, Vermont.

1874—Millard Fillmore dies in Buffalo, New York. Herbert Hoover is born in West Branch, Iowa.

1875—Andrew Johnson dies in Carter's Station, Tennessee.

1876—Colorado enters the Union. "Custer's last stand": he and his men are massacred by Sioux Indians at Little Big Horn, Montana.

1877—Rutherford B. Hayes is elected president as all disputed votes are awarded to him.

1880—James A. Garfield is elected president.

1881—President Garfield is assassinated and dies in Elberon, New Jersey. Vice-President Chester A. Arthur succeeds him.

1882—U.S. bans Chinese immigration. Franklin D. Roosevelt is born in Hyde Park, New York.

1885—Ulysses S. Grant dies in Mount McGregor, New York.

1886—Statue of Liberty is dedicated. Chester A. Arthur dies in New York City.

1888—Benjamin Harrison is elected president.

1889—North Dakota, South Dakota, Washington, and Montana become states.

1890—Dwight D. Eisenhower is born in Denison, Texas. Idaho and Wyoming become states.

1892—Grover Cleveland is elected president.

1893—Rutherford B. Hayes dies in Fremont, Ohio.

1896—William McKinley is elected president. Utah becomes a state.

1898—U.S. declares war on Spain over Cuba.

1899—Philippines demand independence from U.S.

1900—McKinley is reelected. Boxer Rebellion against foreigners in China begins.

1901—McKinley is assassinated by anarchist Leon Czolgosz in Buffalo, New York; Theodore Roosevelt becomes president. Benjamin Harrison dies in Indianapolis, Indiana.

1902—U.S. acquires perpetual control over Panama Canal.

1903—Alaskan frontier is settled.

1904—Russian-Japanese War breaks out. Theodore Roosevelt wins presidential election.

1905—Treaty of Portsmouth signed, ending Russian-Japanese War.

1906—U.S. troops occupy Cuba.

1907—President Roosevelt bars all Japanese immigration. Oklahoma enters the Union.

1908—William Howard Taft becomes president. Grover Cleveland dies in Princeton, New Jersey. Lyndon B. Johnson is born near Stonewall, Texas.

1909—NAACP is founded under W.E.B. DuBois

1910—China abolishes slavery.

1911—Chinese Revolution begins. Ronald Reagan is born in Tampico, Illinois.

1912—Woodrow Wilson is elected president. Arizona and New Mexico become states.

1913—Federal income tax is introduced in U.S. through the Sixteenth Amendment. Richard Nixon is born in Yorba Linda, California. Gerald Ford is born in Omaha, Nebraska.

1914—World War I begins.

1915—British liner *Lusitania* is sunk by German submarine.

1916—Wilson is reelected president.

1917—U.S. breaks diplomatic relations with Germany. Czar Nicholas of Russia abdicates as revolution begins. U.S. declares war on Austria-Hungary. John F. Kennedy is born in Brookline, Massachusetts.

1918—Wilson proclaims "Fourteen Points" as war aims. On November 11, armistice is signed between Allies and Germany.

1919—Eighteenth Amendment prohibits sale and manufacture of intoxicating liquors. Wilson presides over first League of Nations; wins Nobel Peace Prize. Theodore Roosevelt dies in Oyster Bay, New York.

1920—Nineteenth Amendment (women's suffrage) is passed. Warren Harding is elected president.

1921—Adolf Hitler's stormtroopers begin to terrorize political opponents.

1922—Irish Free State is established. Soviet states form USSR. Benito Mussolini forms Fascist government in Italy.

1923—President Harding dies in San Francisco, California; he is succeeded by Vice-President Calvin Coolidge.

1924—Coolidge is elected president. Woodrow Wilson dies in Washington, D.C. James Carter is born in Plains, Georgia. George Bush is born in Milton, Massachusetts.

1925—Hitler reorganizes Nazi Party and publishes first volume of *Mein Kampf.*

1926—Fascist youth organizations founded in Germany and Italy. Republic of Lebanon proclaimed.

1927—Stalin becomes Soviet dictator. Economic conference in Geneva attended by fifty-two nations.

1928—Herbert Hoover is elected president. U.S. and many other nations sign Kellogg-Briand pacts to outlaw war.

1929—Stock prices in New York crash on "Black Thursday"; the Great Depression begins.

1930—Bank of U.S. and its many branches close (most significant bank failure of the year). William Howard Taft dies in Washington, D.C.

1931—Emigration from U.S. exceeds immigration for first time as Depression deepens.

1932—Franklin D. Roosevelt wins presidential election in a Democratic landslide.

1933—First concentration camps are erected in Germany. U.S. recognizes USSR and resumes trade. Twenty-First Amendment repeals prohibition. Calvin Coolidge dies in Northampton, Massachusetts.

1934—Severe dust storms hit Plains states. President Roosevelt passes U.S. Social Security Act.

1936—Roosevelt is reelected. Spanish Civil War begins. Hitler and Mussolini form Rome-Berlin Axis.

1937—Roosevelt signs Neutrality Act.

1938—Roosevelt sends appeal to Hitler and Mussolini to settle European problems amicably.

1939—Germany takes over Czechoslovakia and invades Poland, starting World War II.

1940—Roosevelt is reelected for a third term.

1941—Japan bombs Pearl Harbor, U.S. declares war on Japan. Germany and Italy declare war on U.S.; U.S. then declares war on them.

1942—Allies agree not to make separate peace treaties with the enemies. U.S. government transfers more than 100,000 Nisei (Japanese-Americans) from west coast to inland concentration camps.

1943—Allied bombings of Germany begin.

1944—Roosevelt is reelected for a fourth term. Allied forces invade Normandy on D-Day.

1945—President Franklin D. Roosevelt dies in Warm Springs, Georgia; Vice-President Harry S. Truman succeeds him. Mussolini is killed; Hitler commits suicide. Germany surrenders. U.S. drops atomic bomb on Hiroshima; Japan surrenders: end of World War II.

1946—U.N. General Assembly holds its first session in London. Peace conference of twenty-one nations is held in Paris.

1947—Peace treaties are signed in Paris. "Cold War" is in full swing.

1948—U.S. passes Marshall Plan Act, providing $17 billion in aid for Europe. U.S. recognizes new nation of Israel. India and Pakistan become free of British rule. Truman is elected president.

1949—Republic of Eire is proclaimed in Dublin. Russia blocks land route access from Western Germany to Berlin; airlift begins. U.S., France, and Britain agree to merge their zones of occupation in West Germany. Apartheid program begins in South Africa.

1950—Riots in Johannesburg, South Africa, against apartheid. North Korea invades South Korea. U.N. forces land in South Korea and recapture Seoul.

1951—Twenty-Second Amendment limits president to two terms.

1952—Dwight D. Eisenhower resigns as supreme commander in Europe and is elected president.

1953—Stalin dies; struggle for power in Russia follows. Rosenbergs are executed for espionage.

1954—U.S. and Japan sign mutual defense agreement.

1955—Blacks in Montgomery, Alabama, boycott segregated bus lines.

1956—Eisenhower is reelected president. Soviet troops march into Hungary.

1957—U.S. agrees to withdraw ground forces from Japan. Russia launches first satellite, *Sputnik*.

1958—European Common Market comes into being. Fidel Castro begins war against Batista government in Cuba.

1959—Alaska becomes the forty-ninth state. Hawaii becomes fiftieth state. Castro becomes premier of Cuba. De Gaulle is proclaimed president of the Fifth Republic of France.

1960—Historic debates between Senator John F. Kennedy and Vice-President Richard Nixon are televised. Kennedy is elected president. Brezhnev becomes president of USSR.

1961—Berlin Wall is constructed. Kennedy and Khrushchev confer in Vienna. In Bay of Pigs incident, Cubans trained by CIA attempt to overthrow Castro.

1962—U.S. military council is established in South Vietnam.

1963—Riots and beatings by police and whites mark civil rights demonstrations in Birmingham, Alabama; 30,000 troops are called out, Martin Luther King, Jr., is arrested. Freedom marchers descend on Washington, D.C., to demonstrate. President Kennedy is assassinated in Dallas, Texas; Vice-President Lyndon B. Johnson is sworn in as president.

1964—U.S. aircraft bomb North Vietnam. Johnson is elected president. Herbert Hoover dies in New York City.

1965—U.S. combat troops arrive in South Vietnam.

1966—Thousands protest U.S. policy in Vietnam. National Guard quells race riots in Chicago.

1967—Six-Day War between Israel and Arab nations.

1968—Martin Luther King, Jr., is assassinated in Memphis, Tennessee. Senator Robert Kennedy is assassinated in Los Angeles. Riots and police brutality take place at Democratic National Convention in Chicago. Richard Nixon is elected president. Czechoslovakia is invaded by Soviet troops.

1969—Dwight D. Eisenhower dies in Washington, D.C. Hundreds of thousands of people in several U.S. cities demonstrate against Vietnam War.

1970—Four Vietnam War protesters are killed by National Guardsmen at Kent State University in Ohio.

1971—Twenty-Sixth Amendment allows eighteen-year-olds to vote.

1972—Nixon visits Communist China; is reelected president in near-record landslide. Watergate affair begins when five men are arrested in the Watergate hotel complex in Washington, D.C. Nixon announces resignations of aides Haldeman, Ehrlichman, and Dean and Attorney General Kleindienst as a result of Watergate-related charges. Harry S. Truman dies in Kansas City, Missouri.

1973—Vice-President Spiro Agnew resigns; Gerald Ford is named vice-president. Vietnam peace treaty is formally approved after nineteen months of negotiations. Lyndon B. Johnson dies in San Antonio, Texas.

1974—As a result of Watergate cover-up, impeachment is considered; Nixon resigns and Ford becomes president. Ford pardons Nixon and grants limited amnesty to Vietnam War draft evaders and military deserters.

1975—U.S. civilians are evacuated from Saigon, South Vietnam, as Communist forces complete takeover of South Vietnam.

1976—U.S. celebrates its Bicentennial. James Earl Carter becomes president.

1977—Carter pardons most Vietnam draft evaders, numbering some 10,000.

1980—Ronald Reagan is elected president.

1981—President Reagan is shot in the chest in assassination attempt. Sandra Day O'Connor is appointed first woman justice of the Supreme Court.

1983—U.S. troops invade island of Grenada.

1984—Reagan is reelected president. Democratic candidate Walter Mondale's running mate, Geraldine Ferraro, is the first woman selected for vice-president by a major U.S. political party.

1985—Soviet Communist Party secretary Konstantin Chernenko dies; Mikhail Gorbachev succeeds him. U.S. and Soviet officials discuss arms control in Geneva. Reagan and Gorbachev hold summit conference in Geneva. Racial tensions accelerate in South Africa.

1986—Space shuttle *Challenger* explodes shortly after takeoff; crew of seven dies. U.S. bombs bases in Libya. Corazon Aquino defeats Ferdinand Marcos in Philippine presidential election.

1987—Iraqi missile rips the U.S. frigate *Stark* in the Persian Gulf, killing thirty-seven American sailors. Congress holds hearings to investigate sale of U.S. arms to Iran to finance Nicaraguan *contra* movement.

1988—President Reagan and Soviet leader Gorbachev sign INF treaty, eliminating intermediate nuclear forces. Severe drought sweeps the United States. George Bush is elected president.

1989—East Germany opens Berlin Wall, allowing citizens free exit. Communists lose control of governments in Poland, Romania, and Czechoslovakia. Chinese troops massacre over 1,000 pro-democracy student demonstrators in Beijing's Tiananmen Square.

1990—Iraq annexes Kuwait, provoking the threat of war. East and West Germany are reunited. The Cold War between the United States and the Soviet Union comes to a close. Several Soviet republics make moves toward independence.

1991—Backed by a coalition of members of the United Nations, U.S. troops drive Iraqis from Kuwait. Latvia, Lithuania, and Estonia withdraw from the USSR. The Soviet Union dissolves as its republics secede to form a Commonwealth of Independent States.

1992—U.N. forces fail to stop fighting in territories of former Yugoslavia. More than fifty people are killed and more than six hundred buildings burned in rioting in Los Angeles. U.S. unemployment reaches eight-year high. Hurricane Andrew devastates southern Florida and parts of Louisiana. International relief supplies and troops are sent to combat famine and violence in Somalia.

1993—U.S.-led forces use airplanes and missiles to attack military targets in Iraq. William Jefferson Clinton becomes the forty-second U.S. president.

1994—Richard M. Nixon dies in New York City.

Index

Page numbers in boldface type indicate illustrations.

About the Author

Jane Clark Casey was born in Arkansas in 1947 to James Arthur Carfagno and Rita Maus Carfagno. She attended school in Arkansas, Missouri, and Colorado before settling in Illinois. Her dream of a career as a musical comedy star was tragically ended by the discovery that she could neither sing nor dance. Forced by circumstances to make her living in the law, she now practices with the firm of Winston & Strawn in Chicago. She lives with her husband, Frank, and son, John, who must occasionally remind her not to sing.